You and Me
TOGETHER

Moms, Dads, and Kids Around the World

by Barbara Kerley

with a note by Marian Wright Edelman, President, Children's Defense Fund

NATIONAL GEOGRAPHIC
WASHINGTON, D.C.

Here we are, together.
Together, **ME AND YOU...**

Sharing a **JOKE**

Some SHADE

a RIDE

Playing a **TUNE** *or two*

Taking a **NAP**

a WALK

our time *together*, ME AND YOU

Holding a **HAND**

Telling a **TALE** or two

Making a **MESS**

a **MEAL**

a life *together,* **ME AND YOU**

Catching a **FISH**

a BUS

a BALL

Dancing a **TURN** or two

Seeing the **SUN**

a **STORM**

the world *together,* **ME AND YOU**

You and me together.

Forever, **ME AND YOU.**

Moms, dads, and kids around the WORLD

Arctic Ocean

NORTH AMERICA

Kidafell, Iceland

EUROPE

Berlin, Germany

near Rome, Italy

ASIA

Beijing, China

Kyoto, Japan

Chandos Lake, Ontario, Canada

Germantown, Maryland, U.S.A.

Antelope Canyon, Arizona, U.S.A.

Datil, New Mexico, U.S.A.

Staten Island, New York, U.S.A.

Atlantic Ocean

Paro Valley, Bhutan

Mumbai, Maharashtra, India

Jiddah, Saudi Arabia

Pune, India

Mae Hong Son Province, Thailand

Pacific Ocean

Piñones Beach, Puerto Rico, U.S.A.

Santiago, Guatemala

AFRICA

Pacific Ocean

Paramaribo, Suriname

SOUTH AMERICA

near Kampala, Uganda

Arusha, Tanzania

Goroka, Papua New Guinea

Indian Ocean

Bali, Indonesia

AUSTRALIA

Canta Galo, Rio de Janeiro, Brazil

Uluru National Park, Australia

0   3,000 miles
0   4,000 kilometers

ANTARCTICA

PIÑONES BEACH, PUERTO RICO, U.S.A.
Front cover: A boy takes flight with the help of his father. On this small, tropical island, many families enjoy spending time at the beach. PHOTOGRAPH BY DANA MENUSSI/ GETTY IMAGES

STATEN ISLAND, NEW YORK, U.S.A.
Cooled by ocean breezes, a mother tickles her daughter as they romp together. Staten Island, just south of the Statue of Liberty, is home to many immigrant families. PHOTOGRAPH BY ANNE-MARIE WEBER/ GETTY IMAGES

KIDAFELL, ICELAND
Woolen sweaters warm two children and their mother as they ride near an icy stream. The Icelandic pony has been bred for over a thousand years to have a thick winter coat. PHOTOGRAPH BY DAVE G. HOUSER/CORBIS

DATIL, NEW MEXICO, U.S.A.
A father's lap makes a fine pillow for a tired cowboy. Cattle and sheep are raised on ranches across the state. PHOTOGRAPH BY NATIONAL GEOGRAPHIC PHOTOGRAPHER WILLIAM ALBERT ALLARD

JIDDAH, SAUDI ARABIA
Veiled for modesty, a mother plays with her daughters. Following Muslim custom, the girls may also wear a veil when they are older. PHOTOGRAPH BY NATIONAL GEOGRAPHIC PHOTOGRAPHER JODI COBB

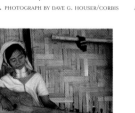

BEIJING, CHINA
A shady spot is the perfect place for a father and son to learn a song. They practice in the park so they won't disturb their neighbors. A classical education in China includes the study of music, board games, calligraphy, and painting. PHOTOGRAPH BY STUART FRANKLIN/MAGNUM PHOTOS

MAE HONG SON PROVINCE, THAILAND
A Padaung mother strums a wooden guitar for her daughter. Traditionally, girls begin to wear brass neck rings when they are five or six years old. PHOTOGRAPH BY CHRIS LISLE/CORBIS

PARO VALLEY, BHUTAN
A son's good company lightens his mother's heavy load. In Bhutan, goods such as firewood and hay may be transported on foot. PHOTOGRAPH BY R. IAN LLOYD/ MASTERFILE

KYOTO, JAPAN

Wearing a traditional hairpiece and clothing, a girl holds her mother's hand. They will celebrate the Festival of Ages, which honors the more than thousand years Kyoto served as Japan's capital. Their costumes reflect the city's rich and varied history. PHOTOGRAPH BY LINC CORNELL/ INDEX STOCK

PUNE, INDIA

A mother and daughter cover each other with colored powder for Holi festival. Celebrating the arrival of spring, Holi is a time to make colorful messes, visit friends, and eat sweets. PHOTOGRAPH COURTESY OF CORBIS

NEAR KAMPALA, UGANDA

Reaching high overhead, children toss a ball with their mother. Although ill with AIDS, their mother enjoys playing ball with her children. PHOTOGRAPH BY LOUISE GUBB/CORBIS SABA

CHANDOS LAKE, ONTARIO, CANADA

A father and son paddle a canoe at day's end. PHOTOGRAPH BY PETER GRIFFITH/MASTERFILE

PARAMARIBO, SURINAME

A daughter joins her mother in celebrating the holiday of Eid al Fitr. After the month-long fast of Ramadan, Muslim families around the world enjoy this day of feasting. PHOTOGRAPH BY ROBERT CAPUTO/ AURORA

ARUSHA, TANZANIA

In the shadow of Longido Mountain, a boy stands next to his father, holding a pet goat. Raising livestock—cattle, sheep, and goats—is an important part of Maasai culture. PHOTOGRAPH BY ALISON WRIGHT/ CORBIS

NEAR ROME, ITALY

Two girls wait patiently for their mother to finish cooking. For Gypsy, or Roma, families who are traditionally on the move, a kitchen can be anyplace with a good, hot fire. PHOTOGRAPH BY DAVID TURNLEY/ CORBIS

GERMANTOWN, MARYLAND, U.S.A.

A daughter's toes are safe when she stands atop her father's big, black shoes. The waltz, popular in Europe during the 19th Century, is still enjoyed today. PHOTOGRAPH BY DANIEL R. WESTERGREN, NATIONAL GEOGRAPHIC SOCIETY

GOROKA, PAPUA NEW GUINEA

Asaro fathers and sons, made up as "Mudmen," come together for the annual sing-sing. Families from all over the country meet to share tribal songs and dances. PHOTOGRAPH BY NATIONAL GEOGRAPHIC PHOTOGRAPHER JODI COBB

BALI, INDONESIA

A father and son carry rakes as they walk through a rice field. Much of the work of growing rice, a staple crop in Southeast Asia, is done by hand. PHOTOGRAPH BY JACK FIELDS/CORBIS

CANTA GALO, RIO DE JANEIRO, BRAZIL

A father and son enjoy an afternoon of fishing on a quiet lake. The fish they catch may be prepared with tomatoes, peppers, and coconut milk in a dish called *moqueca*. PHOTOGRAPH BY SILVESTRE MACHADO/ GETTY IMAGES

ANTELOPE CANYON, ARIZONA, U.S.A.

A mother and daughter find a shaft of sunlight through the red-rock walls of a slot canyon. Cut into the sandstone bedrock by centuries of wind and rain, the canyon is in some spots only three feet wide. PHOTOGRAPH BY PAUL DAMIEN/NGS IMAGE COLLECTION

ULURU NATIONAL PARK, AUSTRALIA

Back cover: Watching his father carefully, an Aborigine son learns how to carve a boomerang. Once completed, it can be used in ceremonies or for hunting. PHOTOGRAPH BY RICHARD T. NOWITZ/CORBIS

SANTIAGO, GUATEMALA

A father and son swap stories on a sunny day. Maya culture includes a rich tradition of storytelling. PHOTOGRAPH BY FRANS LEMMENS/ GETTY IMAGES

BERLIN, GERMANY

Wearing a bright red hat for the outing, a daughter smiles with her father as they watch the world pass by. PHOTOGRAPH BY GEOFFREY CLIFFORD/GETTY IMAGES

MUMBAI, MAHARASHTRA, INDIA

Monsoon rains wash over a mother and her daughter as they walk together. Based on the Arabic word *mawsim*, this "season" of winds brings rainy weather to much of South Asia. PHOTOGRAPH BY JAGDISH AGARWAL/ SCPHOTOS/ALAMY IMAGES

A note on *the world's* CHILDREN

Parents love their children, and children love their parents. As this magical collection of photographs and words makes

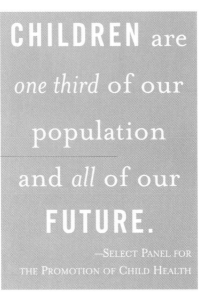

CHILDREN are *one third* of our population and *all* of our **FUTURE.**

—Select Panel for the Promotion of Child Health

abundantly clear, parents and children find joy in each other day in and day out, over meals and at play, sharing work, making music, while dancing and praying—or just being together. Love between parents and children is universal, and we see it shining here from Tanzania to Germany, from Bhutan to New Mexico. Our children are precious. But for many children of this world, love alone does not sustain them. Worse, for some children of this world, love is not even familiar.

Yes, parents love their children, but we need a world of parents who love *all* children. We need parents who will not just take the hand of their own child but will offer a helping hand to a community and nation of children. We need parents

who will not just read to a daughter before bedtime but who will raise insistent voices for education for a generation of girls in places where learning is lacking or saved only for boys. We need parents who will not just listen to the dreams of a single son but who will realize the right of every child with whom that son must share a world to pursue a dream.

Why have we endangered so badly the hopes and lives of so many children? What kind of world permits 38,000 children to die every day from preventable poverty-related causes? What kind of world lets children and mothers die in violent wars

CELEBRATING TOGETHER: *A daughter joins her mother in prayer on the Muslim holiday of Eid al Fitr. Children begin learning the customs and cultures of their countries from their parents.*

and massacres? What kind of rich nation like America lets a child be abused or neglected every 11 seconds; be born into poverty every 40 seconds; and be killed by guns every 3 hours? We must never adjust to an unjust world which lets children die needlessly. We must pray, persevere, and refuse to give up. We must open our eyes and our hearts and energize and organize so that all children in all places in our borderless world—in Africa and South America, in Australia and Europe, in North America, and all over the world—have what they need. Let us push our love beyond the children in our own homes to give all children a home in the world of our hearts.

> Our *greatest* natural resource is the *minds* of our **CHILDREN.**
> —WALT DISNEY

Dietrich Bonhoeffer, the great German theologian who died opposing Hitler's Holocaust, said, "The test of the morality of a society is what it does for its children." It's time for the U.S. and all the nations of the world to pass Bonhoeffer's test.

Let us make a new world for our children beginning today. *We can.*

Let us set a goal of ending child poverty and neglect in the richest, most powerful nation on earth by 2010. *We can.*

Let us commit to meet the United Nations millennium goal on poverty, child health, and girls' education. *We can.*

Let us change the priorities of our world so weapons of mass destruction are transformed into weapons of life: peace, health, clean air and water, and rich cultures. *We can.*

Who will do this? We will. You and me. *You and me together.*

> **MANKIND** owes to the *child* the **BEST** it has to give.
> —UNITED NATIONS CONVENTION ON THE RIGHTS OF THE CHILD

MARIAN WRIGHT EDELMAN
President, Children's Defense Fund

For **ANN, BILL, JULIA,** and **ALEC:**

loved a million worlds.

Published by the National Geographic Society.

All rights reserved. Reproduction of the whole or any part of the contents
without written permission from the National Geographic Society is strictly prohibited.

With special thanks to Jennifer Emmett and Bea Jackson.

If you would like to learn more about the Children's Defense Fund or find out how you can help the movement to Leave No Child Behind® visit:
http://www.childrensdefense.org or call 202 628-8787.

Book Designer: Bea Jackson
Illustrations Editor: Janet Dustin
The text of the book is set in Mrs. Eaves and Trade Gothic.

Library of Congress Cataloging-in-Publication Data
Kerley, Barbara.
You and Me Together : Moms, Dads, and Kids Around the World / By Barbara Kerley.
p. cm.
1. Parent and child—Juvenile literature. I. Title.
HQ755.85.K46 2005
306.874—dc22
2004007079
Trade Edition ISBN 0-7922-8297-3   Library Edition ISBN 0-7922-8298-1

The world's largest nonprofit scientific and educational organization, the National Geographic Society was founded in 1888
"for the increase and diffusion of geographic knowledge." Since then it has supported scientific exploration
and spread information to its more than eight million members worldwide.

The National Geographic Society educates and inspires millions every day through magazines, books, television programs, videos, maps and atlases,
research grants, the National Geographic Bee, teacher workshops, and innovative classroom materials. The Society is supported through membership
dues, charitable gifts, and income from the sale of its educational products. Members receive NATIONAL GEOGRAPHIC magazine—the Society's official
journal—discounts on Society products and other benefits. For more information about the National Geographic Society, its educational programs
and publications, and ways to support its work, please call 1-800-NGS-LINE (647-5463) or write to the following address:

NATIONAL GEOGRAPHIC SOCIETY
1145 17th Street N.W.
Washington, D.C. 20036-4688 U.S.A.
Visit the Society's Web site: www.nationalgeographic.com

PRINTED IN THE UNITED STATES OF AMERICA

06-984